I0559274

A BIRD WITH
A Broken Wing

A BIRD WITH A Broken Wing

CARE GIVING

DR. SHARON FORDE-ATIKOSSIE

CITI OF
BOOKS

Copyright © 2024 by Dr. Sharon Forde-Atikossie

All rights reserved. No part of this publication may be reproduced, distributed, or transmitted in any form or by any means, including photocopying, recording, or other electronic or mechanical methods, without the prior written permission of the copyright owner and the publisher, except in the case of brief quotations embodied in critical reviews and certain other noncommercial uses permitted by copyright law. For permission requests, write to the publisher, addressed "Attention: Permissions Coordinator," at the address below.

CITIOFBOOKS, INC.
3736 Eubank NE Suite A1
Albuquerque, NM 87111-3579
www.citiofbooks.com
Hotline: 1 (877) 389-2759
Fax: 1 (505) 930-7244

Ordering Information:
Quantity sales. Special discounts are available on quantity purchases by corporations, associations, and others. For details, contact the publisher at the address above.

Printed in the United States of America.

ISBN-13: Softcover   978-1-962366-99-1
         eBook   978-1-963209-21-1

Library of Congress Control Number: 2024900520

Dear Readers,

I hope what I have written brings some form of comfort to you, especially in the case of losing your spouse, your partner, or another loved one.

I want you to know you are not alone in this situation, for death comes suddenly and unexpectedly regardless of whether the person is ill or expected to die soon.

It simultaneously comes as a surprise and a shock, not forgetting the confusion and unexplained feeling of "I cannot believe this is happening" that comes to mind.

All because we never know when that time will come; nothing will make sense, and one cannot function properly. Also, many questions fill one's mind, and the main one is, "What am I going to do?"

Nothing will seem easy after that fateful day; it brings feelings of sorrow and loss and every time you hear of someone passing, a sadness comes over you, and the memory of your loved one comes to mind as fresh as the day they died.

One thing I can say is that to survive this ordeal, we must learn to cope with the situation, which is easier said than done.

I pray that God blesses you with peace of mind and gives you the strength to endure the pain you are going through, for I know it is not easy.

I got involved with various activities to cope. I listened to gospel and secular songs that would have me laughing instead of crying, watched movies, including children's cartoons, traveled a little bit, surrounded myself with a positive environment, and, best of all, glued myself to my prayer partner, and by so doing my focus shifted from the death and memory of my love. In MOST cases, this brought peace to my heart.

Despite it all, when you think you are by yourself, understand that you are not alone, and remember that God does not give us more than we can bear!

Sincerely,

Dr. Sharon Forde-Atikossie

Foreword

A Bird with a Broken Wing by Dr. Sharon Forde-Atikossie is an intense book for those who have lost a close loved one.

It is profoundly moving and deeply insightful with her personal experiences with death and the grieving process, which many of us can relate to. It is also raw and unflinching.

This book speaks of things that some of us would not dream of mentioning for fear of embarrassment.

The author speaks very candidly about herself and highlights many topics I have not read about or heard of before, and I am still experiencing most of the things stated in the book.

Even though this book brought tears to my eyes and a little pain to my heart, it also gave me joy. It has eased my pain to a point, allowing me to understand that I am not alone in this grieving process and that many others are experiencing the same things that Dr. Forde-Atikossie experienced.

The boldness in her writing shows the pain she endured, and her desire to share it with us allowed me to look at myself with a better understanding of how I should look at my loved one's death. I try to remember what they did when they were alive, which I see as the season they had on earth, and to think of their lifespan as a legacy they left behind.

This book is a compelling and intense read which, in the end, makes one smile and begin to come to terms with reality and wanting to cope with the death of a loved one.

It makes one want to live rather than wallow in self-pity.

Mrs. Violet Gaskin

Dedication

To the United Churches Fellowship Church family, Pastor Sandra Manning, Faith and Love Center Pentecostal, The Arthur Family, the Grace Tabernacle Church family, the Atikossie family, my sons, some of my military veteran friends, my prayer partner, and not forgetter my sister in Christ Mother Mattie Bowman, and newfound friend Brian Jenkins for walking beside me as I cope, and still dealing with the loss of my husband, Sewayedu R. Atikossie.

I am grateful to God for placing you all in my life!

Dr. Sharon Forde-Atikossie

Acknowledgments

A Bird with a Broken Wing focuses on a personal experience with death and gives an extraordinary insight into how I initially began to cope and am still dealing with the absence of my husband, who is no longer standing by my side. I recognize and acknowledge you, the reader.

Plenty of people helped bring this book to fruition, and I am very grateful to all of them for their support.

First, I must give honor to my God for bringing me through, and by faith, I know He will continue to guide me through this process as I go through my everyday life.

To the Faith and Love Center Pentecostal Center Church that embraced my family and me and continues to cover us with prayers as we endure our loss.

To the United Churches Fellowship Church family, which constantly sends out notifications to pray and support not only me and my family but also everyone else.

To the Arthur Family, the rock I am always holding on to. They make sure we want for nothing.

To the Grace Tabernacle Church family, which embraces me and keeps me laughing.

To the close-knit Atikossie family, who has a family member calling daily to make sure we are okay and constantly reminding us that we are serving an awesome God.

My sons took time out of their busy schedules to check on me.

Some of my homeless military veteran friends, whom I met at Chosen300 Ministry, always have good words of encouragement for me.

My prayer partner, who shall remain nameless, who prayers with me daily.

My sister in Christ, Mother Mattie Bowman, who always walks beside me, making sure that I get out of bed even when I am grumbling, who makes sure that I always have a companion, and who is 'a true caregiver.'

My newfound friend Rev Brian Jenkins, 'The Chicken man from Chosen300,' who disregarded what many would say and became a true confidant, who embraced and tolerated our friendship, and, thereby, opened the doors of his ministry to accommodate me and our ministry, The Sharing of Bread International Outreach Ministry, to work side by side.

Table of Contents

Introduction

I scanned my surroundings as I sat on the stairs of my home, which I shared with my husband, my two sons, and, of course, my grandbaby London (my Boobo Bear). As I looked at the trees and the gradual improvements the neighbors had made to the exterior of their homes, I became distracted by a movement in the sky, and my eyes turned to see a bird calmly soaring above my head, or so I thought.

Within seconds, the bird dropped to the ground, barely avoiding being crushed by a passing car. Yes, I watched the bird fall to the ground, and honestly, I thought and felt nothing about it at that moment. I totally ignored what had just occurred as I continued to admire my surroundings.

Suddenly, out of curiosity, my eyes returned to the bird fluttering on the road, and I was aware that I should have felt some form of guilt, but I did not.

I merely got up and went to the bird, thinking I did not want to see another car drive past and smash it to bits.

I intended to push it out of the way with my foot. I know this may seem cruel, but let us be honest; most of us would have done the same.

However, as I walked over to the bird and saw how it was struggling a sudden guilt came over me, and all I could see was this bird struggling to fly. I noticed that one of its wings was bent backward, and the bird seemed helpless.

I picked the bird up and, honestly, in my annoyance, began to place the bird on one of the neighbor's lawns, planning to walk away, but I could not bring myself to do so after observing its helplessness.

I began to examine it and realized that its right wing was broken, and a few moments of sadness came over me.

While looking at the bird in my hands, I felt like I had a broken wing, too.

The bird was by itself, and here I was by myself, and the thought that came to mind was, "This bird's wing will be healed; will my heart heal?"

I handled the bird very gently and took it into the house in the hope that I could mend its wing, and after a few bits of pecking and scratches and feeding it a few pieces of bread, it became my friend.

After placing one of my grandbaby's popsicle sticks on her wing and tying it with some strong yarn, she stopped fighting, and I sensed a mutual trust had formed between us at that moment.

After a couple of days of feeding and petting, including a bit of massaging on its wings, I placed the bird outside my home with the intent that she may fly away, but she (my little Keba) did not.

Little Keba kept testing her wings by flying around a little at a time, and then she would pass and chirp at the same time, then Keba would fly away and stay away for more extended periods at a time, then one day, she showed up and sat on the fence in the front yard, and then began walking up and down.

I walked through the door with a piece of bread in my hands, stretching it toward her, and hesitated. Then, she took it and suddenly flew away with a loud chirp.

As I looked at her flying away, chirping with the popsicle stick still tied to her wing, I noticed the awkwardness of her flying, but she seemed happy and flew away without returning. At that moment, I sensed it was her last visit.

Now, there I was, watching the bird with a broken wing flying away. She was healed and could fly despite the awkwardness. As I stood up and looked to the sky, thinking about the bird and how happy she was to return to her world, the thought came to my mind, "She is healed. Not to perfection, but she can fly. Will I be able to fly with joy like that little bird with its broken wing?"

Comparing my life to the bird allowed me to think seriously about myself and the hurt and pain I was enduring, which did not seem to be going away.

I began to remember that fateful day when I became Keba (the bird with a broken wing) after receiving the call, "No, Mama, he has not woken up from sleep."

My first thoughts were, "What am I going to do? What is going to happen to me? Who is going to take care of me?" A crippling loneliness came over me, including a feeling of numbness, disbelief, and shock.

I felt lost, confused, and shocked simultaneously. God, my buddy, my covering, my life string was yanked away from me.

Who was I going to fuss with, who was going to talk to me, who was going to stroke my neck when I returned from a hard day's work? Who was going to understand me? What was I going to do now he had left me? Why did he do this to me? It was me, me, me!

I was reflecting on myself only rather than thinking about what my husband endured, which was a daily dose of pain. This may sound selfish, but this feeling was because we had spent one of our best days of laughter together, and I did not want it to end. I was comfortable in my skin and did not want it to change.

My husband had woken up that morning with a burst of energy and begun walking from the bedroom to the kitchen and even went outside the house and walked to the front of the yard. He did that about three times, and he was praising God and thanking Him because he was feeling no pain, and I was there alongside him, also thanking God. For thirteen years, my husband was never without pain, and the average amount of sleep we got was about four hours nightly.

I was praising and thanking God because our worrying was over, and my exact words were, "Thank God, my husband is healed." I was looking forward to us enjoying ourselves and, of course, in my selfish nature, to getting a better night's sleep.

During the day, he did as he always did. He called all his family members, talking, laughing, and reading the Bible. After reaching out to many people, there began an influx of calls from his brothers in Christ; about seven of them called and talked to him, and the conversations all ended with a prayer. Especially with a brother called Deacon Bowman; that was the last call he received.

I became a little suspicious during this time, and I asked my husband why all the calls. I asked him, "Why are these people calling you?" It did not make any sense to me because this was the first time this had ever occurred.

He responded with a smile and said they were rejoicing with him.

My husband listened to gospel songs and preached throughout the day, and his last words were, "Sharon, the word of God is so powerful."

Then, our oldest son came knocking at the door, and I heard him calling out, "Dad!! Dad!!" And I kept saying, "Your dad is fine," and he said, "No, Mom, Dad is not fine."

I walked to my husband, who was sitting in the chair smiling with his headphones on his ears. I sat next to him and held him in my arms, and his body went limp like a rag doll.

I kept begging him to wake up, but all I could see was that peaceful smile on his face, and he was not responding to me. It was as if he was in another world. Then, my son came and held me and placed my husband on the floor at my feet while at the same time talking to someone on the phone. (That is a memory I would not want to relive.)

Everything around me reminded me of my husband after his death, and I soon learned that this type of situation occurs, especially if you live with that person for a long time.

There is that intimacy shared because of doing things together and understanding each other, and when that is gone, there are feelings of loneliness and being alone.

My husband and I read the Bible together most days, and there was never a dull moment in the home when we were discussing the Word of God. We would try to anticipate what next subject matter our Bishop or whoever would be preaching the next Sunday would preach about.

We did most things together except shopping, which he loved, and I was the same. We sometimes reached home having purchased the same type of items, and regardless of where he was or which country we were in, we made sure we reached out to each other, and he would say, "Do not forget what the Bishop said and don't stop praying," and in return, I would say something clever, and we would laugh.

Do not get me wrong. We fought, at least I quarreled, and he went quiet, and we had reached a point in our lives where even when we were angry at each other for something or the other, we would still ask each other if we wanted or needed something to eat or drink.

I saw myself as a bird with two wings. I could fly, and then, suddenly, one of my wings was broken.

I was a woman with a husband, two adopted boys, and a beautiful, feisty granddaughter, and suddenly, in the blink of an eye, the family of five became a family of four.

My husband's body went limp in my arms, and later, he was taken to the hospital and never returned home. Despite the fact I knew he was gone, never to return home, for some time, I felt as if he was on one of those mini vacations he used to take to see his relatives and would burst through the door at any moment to tell me he was hungry with a grin on his face, and then there is that reality check. He is never coming back home.

I was a married woman who had mainly couples as friends. Suddenly, I was classified as a widow whose only life for about fifteen years had been surrounded by only my husband and children. The only outings we had taken were attending church and visiting families.

A woman whose friends were all couples, who used to visit each other's homes, and suddenly felt uncomfortable around them because it was me alone. This is not to say I did not try. Still, when visiting, I felt uncomfortable because of the constant questions like, "Are you okay?" It was evident there was no trust among the women.

I noticed some women's smiles and acknowledgment toward me were different as they clinched onto their husbands' arms.

Some couples welcomed me with open arms; they went to the extent of inviting me to their homes and went beyond that in sending their spouses to assist me. Today, they have become my brothers and sisters, and I claim their families as my own.

Grief/Coping with Grief

It is not easy to lose your spouse or the love of your life. Many changes take place at the same time, and many questions come to mind. I learned there are no wrong or right ways when it comes to grief and that one will endure many types and stages. The event is very significant and one of life's biggest challenges.

After my spouse's death, I was advised on so many things regarding what to do, what not to do, who to call, who not to call, who to talk to, and who to stay away from. All of this was to eliminate the feeling of hurt I was enduring and to work back to having normalcy in my life.

However, I soon learned that everyone grieves differently, and there is no one way to grieve because everyone's situation is different.

I visited many grief groups and listened to many explanations about what defines grief, the different types of grief, the stages of grief, and the difference between grief and depression. I visited a divorcee group and a singles group; desperate times call for desperate measures.

Each group spoke mainly of loneliness and how to overcome it. Some spoke on the stages of pain and, if not careful, how easily depression can step in. One thing I was looking for was how to feel so the pain would go away.

The feeling of acute pain still lingers to this day, and it emerges especially when visiting families, places where my husband and I went as a couple, or places where he shopped. I remember the things we shared and think of him physically, especially in the intimate sense, remembering his smile, the things he used to say, his encouraging words, how he made me laugh, and how he knew me well enough to calm me down.

I soon realized there is no one way of grieving. It has no shame and no boundaries. It has its own path. It has no timetable, and if not careful, grief can control one to the point where one is not only grieving but developing feelings of life-threatening, self-neglect and suicidal thoughts. It also causes one's immune system to be disrupted and feelings that lead to depression.

The APA Dictionary of Psychology explains that 'Grief often includes physiological distress, separation anxiety, confusion, yearning, obsessive dwelling on the past, and apprehension about the future.'

Intense grief can become life-threatening through the disruption of the immune system, self-neglect, and suicidal thoughts, and it may also take the form of regret for something lost, remorse for something done, or sorrow for a mishap to oneself.

I learned that there are five to seven stages of grief, and the full list is denial, anger, bargaining, depression, acceptance, shock, and hope.

The stages of grief are real, and I can say I have experienced them all from the time my husband died to today.

Denial, I learned afterward, temporarily helped me cope with my husband's traumatic death, but eventually, reality kicked in. Denial allowed me to avoid the truth, at least for a short time. It is known to be a defense mechanism that can help minimize the pain, like that I felt when my husband died.

However, I reached a point where I had a reality check that led to the knowledge, "My husband is not going to return home to me."

My anger was two-fold. I was angry because my husband was dead; he was not coming back from the hospital, and I would not see him anymore. He had been taken away from me too soon by the man I loved (my God), and I felt cheated. I was angry because my comfort zone was no longer there, and worst of all, there was nothing I could do.

I wanted to lash out at God for taking my husband because, on the last day of my husband's life, He gave me a precious gift to remember. We spent my husband's last day together, laughing and enjoying ourselves.

I was surely looking forward to more, for that day was unexplained. The moment I began to try and understand, I had to stop myself because only God knows the reason why he died. I am in no position to question or exercise any type of authority when it comes to Him.

Sabrina Romina (PSYD) explained that bargaining is a defense against the feelings of helplessness experienced after a loss. It occurs when people struggle to accept the reality of the loss and the limits of their control over the situation.

I was more focused on why God took my husband, and I was not going to bargain with anyone, knowing I may or may not keep any promises.

According to the APA Dictionary of Psychology, depression is a common mental disorder that causes a persistent feeling of sadness and loss of interest in activities. It can affect how one feels, thinks, and behaves and can lead to various emotional and physical problems.

It is a feeling of sadness and low energy, poor sleep, and emotional reactions. It brings feelings of loneliness, which can soon become emotional numbness, and not forgetting these types of feelings can lead toward suicide.

I experienced all the above symptoms, and to be honest, I am still experiencing them. I sometimes feel so drained that all I want to do is go and sleep and not wake up. My mind tells me to get up, but as I lay there, my body says no.

Sometimes, I feel lost and begin to think of things that cause me to experience severe headaches, including feelings of having my back to the wall and a knot in my stomach, which sometimes makes me feel like I can't breathe.

A healthy acceptance of death can mean a person comes to terms with their mortality and lives their life in personally fulfilling and meaningful ways without fear of death or dying.

In my opinion, acceptance of death is when an individual recognizes and accepts the fact that their loved one is dead. Amen!

This is not easy to come to terms with, especially if you were very close to that loved one. For me, it will be a while before I accept my husband's death.

It is still difficult to cope with, so acceptance may come later in life.

Shock manifests when one has no reaction to the news of losing a loved one. This is when one cannot believe the person is gone.

According to the Bible dictionary, hope is looking forward to a positive outcome; it is the desire to have something good in the future, a feeling of expectation, and a desire or wish for something. According to the dictionary, hope is to cherish a desire with anticipation.

According to the Bible in Romans 8:24-25 and Hebrews 11:1,7, hope is a fundamental component of the life of the righteous.

What is hope if I cannot get what I want? And that is to see my husband walking through the door, smiling at me.

Now, I must seek an alternative where hope is a concern, and that is to be happy, remember my husband, and still live a normal life.

It seems impossible, and to be honest, I know I will be healed by the grace of God, with or without perfection.

That is my hope: to be healed and have peace of mind. Regardless of what may occur, I will remember and grieve for him, knowing now that a process of grief must take place.

There are various depths to grief, and it all depends on the level of closeness and the love one had for the one who is gone.

For me, when I compared the loss of my brother, dad, husband, aunts, cousins, and even a friend, I found that initially, intense disdainful feelings lingered in my heart.

The pain was beyond my control, and I could do nothing to stop it, not for the sake of not trying. Regardless of who the person is, some form of emotion comes over us, which allows us to feel hurt.

Different types of pain when death occurs

When I compared the pain when my dad died or my brother's death to my husband's, they all seemed different.

The common denominator of all three losses was the pain, including the feeling that part of me had been yanked away.

My brother, Michael, was the eldest of five children, and I was the third in the bunch. We all loved each other but had different friends and interests, and our closeness was due to us living in the same home, seeing each other often, and having to wrestle with each other for something or the other.

The thought of not seeing him again caused me such pain that I cried for about three days. At that time, I found comfort in the arms of a friend who tried to find many ways to keep me occupied and to overcome his death, but despite it all, his memory still lingers in me even though it has been over forty years now, and, yes, tears still come sometimes.

I learned to cope with his death, which allowed me to get closer to his children and grandchildren. It is not for me to get closer to them to remind them of who I am, but a little selfishly to keep a calmness and a smile on my face.

In my dad's case, even though he did not live with us for long, a part of me always loved him, but the closeness I shared with my brother was deeper than with my dad.

I remember my dad with fondness; his smile and the way he would put me on his bicycle and take me for a ride, which I later found out was his way of getting rid of me. However, when I listen to some of my associates talk about their dads, the things they did with them, and how they look forward to spending more time with them, I sometimes feel a little jealous, but I soon get over it because I love seeing people happy.

When it came to my husband, the emotion built up in me in such a way that sometimes, I couldn't breathe. His memory lingers in me nonstop, and usually, the pain is so severe that I can't function. We spent most of fifteen years together, and we had reached that point where we would complete each other's sentences and know what each other was about to say.

I learned that coping with death is vital to one's mental health, for it is natural to experience grief when a loved one dies, and the best thing to do is allow oneself to grieve. It is advised that grieving people seek out caring people to cope effectively with the pain, including friends and relatives who can understand your feelings of loss or who have experienced a similar loss. Another way is to join supportive groups and share with others who are experiencing similar losses, including grief groups, counseling groups, and other groups one feels comfortable with.

Express your feelings by telling others how you feel and managing your grief. This can help one work through the grieving process.

Take care of your health by maintaining regular contact with your family physician and ensuring you eat well and get plenty of rest.

Accept that life is for the living by trying to begin to live again in the present and not dwelling on the past.

Postpone major life changes, including moving, remarrying, changing jobs, or having another child. Give yourself time to adjust to your loss.

I was patient; it can take months or even years to absorb a significant loss and accept your changed life.

Seek outside help when necessary. If your grief seems too much to bear, seek professional assistance to help work through it. Seeking help is a sign of strength, not weakness.

I do not want to be bothered

I did not want to hear anyone mention my husband's name or speak of him. Because of this, I did not want to study the word of God with anyone who knew him, and I went to the extent of asking for a recommendation from our church's Bishop to identify someone to study with who did not know my husband.

Many people call my home and cell phone, and sometimes, I will answer their calls, and sometimes, I will not answer the phone, for I know for sure I will cry, and that feeling of despair will come all over again.

Conversely, when it came to his brothers and family, I wanted to call and talk to them but decided against it because I did not want them to feel the pain that I was feeling.

When looking at this situation, no one wanted to call for fear of reigniting the pain in the other, so I had to be careful of my behavior because there would be a time when I would need them.

Sometimes, I would look at an item that belonged to my husband, and the feeling of hurt would come over me; in another instant, I would look at or touch something that belonged to him and feel nothing.

Sometimes, I would lay in bed awake, and the tears would continuously roll down my face, and in another instant, my eyes were wide open all night, and I would either stare into space or not think about anything.

Other times, something would come to mind, and I would begin laughing, smiling, or even arguing as if my husband were in the house with me.

I would lay in bed for days without bathing or eating and refusing to accept calls.

Advice Received

Most of those who had lost loved ones gave advice, especially women. Some people advised me on who to talk to and who not to talk to, and all the advice, regardless of how ridiculous it sounded, was well received by me because I honestly did not know what I was doing.

I really wanted to be happy and not sad. However, I soon learned that everyone grieves differently, and what would have worked for them may not have worked for me. My priority was not to be sad or hurt because the pain was too much, and I knew that I had to live and make sure it was done correctly and to suit my needs.

Some people advised me to talk about his death to my loved ones and friends, which would help me understand what happened to my husband. I tried that, and every time, I ended up sad than ever. All the people seemed sincere, but after a while, they seemed bored. I feel this type of conversation should be left to the experts and counselors.

Some people encouraged me to accept my feelings, and I must say I grew worse and sad, and all I wanted was for my husband to come home to me.

Reaching out and helping others who were dealing with their loss was another disaster for me. I was thinking more about my situation than those I was supposed to be helping. I found each of us had a different type of relationship with our spouses, and the only things we all had in common were that we had a loss, we were hurting, and our loved ones were not returning home.

Some did not get the opportunity to say goodbye, and their pain seemed beyond repair. For others, their loved ones seemed to be trying to talk to them before their deaths, and they could not understand what was being said. This pain caused them to become desperate in wanting to know what their loved one was saying.

A very thought-out piece of advice was for me to take care of myself and my family; I did this and continue to do so, and I am trying to continue to take care of myself the best way I know how with the help of others.

Remembering to celebrate life is a work in progress. It is not as easy as it sounds. I had to learn to accept my husband's passing, and all I know is that I lost him, and nothing else matters. Whose life am I celebrating?

Maybe in time, but I give my God thanks and praise for blessing me. Since I do not know why He took my husband, I have no choice but to accept it and know that God had a plan for both him and me, and I am beginning to learn to celebrate what is in front of me and accept what God is doing in my life.

Permitting myself to feel is a daily chore I go through. I deal with this every day, allowing myself to let the tears flow, regardless of what I am doing.

Distracting myself from the hurt and pain does work for a bit; when I am happy, I stop thinking about anything else and focus on the situation at hand, but after the work or whatever I am doing is finished, the hurt and pain are still there, and the void is only filled for a few hours.

Distraction does not work when it comes to easing the pain of death; it is just a temporary fix. This situation becomes a roller coaster, and the pain never disappears.

Breaking Down

I use the words 'breaking down' deliberately because that is precisely how it felt when hearing someone speaking my husband's name. When I met someone who had not heard of my husband's death, I had to summon up the courage to tell them that he was no longer alive, and the memory of that fateful day replayed in my mind all over again.

Having to change his name on documents was terrible. It was not easy to present a death certificate at my employment or change the name on the vehicle or properties. The reminders of my husband's death and the pain lasted for days after such an activity, and this affected not only my job but all other situations in my life.

When this happened, the feeling became real, and realizing my husband was not coming home again caused a tightness in my stomach or a longing for his presence, lingering in my mind for a long time.

Saying the words, "He has passed on," was very difficult, especially at functions where people were expecting him to accompany me.

I had difficulty in visiting the stores and shopping areas that we visited together. I felt self-conscious and prayed no one recognized me.

Waking up during the night was another painful experience. This happened sporadically, and I would be awake all night without feeling sleepy and then able to function the next day without any form of distraction.

"Where is the pastor? I want to talk to him."

"You came by yourself. Is the pastor okay?" I heard these statements when traveling internationally to do our mission activities.

I would walk toward someone, and they would look over my shoulder. I soon realized they were expecting my husband.

Working on projects that my husband was working on was hard. My husband and I worked together to get things done most of the time, and many of those projects still need to be completed. When it was time to do so, I couldn't seem to get it right, and in the end, finding someone else to complete it was the best approach.

Smelling the food my husband liked was another hurt, and to ease my pain, I avoided restaurants with that smell, at least for a while.

Discarding my loved one's personal items was incredibly difficult. I did not want to let go, but gradually, I began releasing some of his things. However, I am still holding on to many. I feel at this point that time heals all wounds.

It is very hard to give anything away, especially when getting rid of the belongings of someone who has passed away. Sometimes, some of the loved one's items or property can be easily discarded, but other times, one may want to hold on to something as simple as a pen. Seeing all my husband's things sometimes grieved my heart to the point where I wanted to scream.

A pain would wash over me every time I decided to get rid of my husband's belongings, and there was an accompanying feeling of greed. I did not want to give away anything that belonged to my husband, especially his hats and colognes.

The thought of someone else wearing his clothes angered me, and this is one reason why it is better to allow others to take your loved one's clothes and belongings away.

The Feelings of Loneliness

When loneliness steps in, it comes with hurt, pain, and distractions; nothing can take that feeling away until calmness returns.

Sometimes, you can feel your loved one is in the home with you. I would find myself sometimes smiling, and within an instant, I would begin to cry because the reality that he was not on vacation and would never be walking through the door humming out-of-tune would lay back across my shoulders.

The church we attended is behind our home, and that is harder to deal with. Not only attending the same church but also remembering he used to regularly visit the back of the church, and I could always hear him doing something there. I would always pass some form of beverage over the fence to him and whomever he was with at the time.

It is not easy climbing the stairs to the pulpit and passing the area where my husband's head was last laid.

Coping with Grief and Loss

Grief is personal, and I am not ashamed of how I feel. It is normal to grieve for the loss I experienced. There are various healthy ways to cope with the intense pain that can ease sadness and help me come to terms with my kind of loss, finding new meanings about why I experienced my loss with the aim of moving on with my life.

My life will never be the same after losing my husband, but in time, my pain will ease, and then I will start looking to the future and eventually come to terms with my loss.

The grieving process takes time, and it depends on the person. I learned there is no right or wrong way to grieve, and it depends on your personality and coping style, your life experience, your faith, and how significant the loss was to you.

I learned that grieving is the outward expression of one's loss. It can be expressed physically, emotionally, and psychologically. For instance, crying is a physical expression, while depression is psychological. It is vital to allow yourself to express these feelings.

At first, it may seem helpful to separate yourself from the pain, but you cannot avoid grieving forever. Someday, those feelings must be resolved, or they may cause physical or emotional illness.

Many people report physical symptoms accompanying grief. Stomach pain, loss of appetite, intestinal upsets, sleep disturbances, and loss of energy are all common symptoms of acute grief. Of all life's stresses, mourning can seriously test your natural defense systems. Existing illnesses may worsen, or new conditions may develop.

Profound emotional reactions may occur. These reactions include anxiety attacks, chronic fatigue, depression, and thoughts of suicide. An obsession with the deceased is also a common reaction to death.

There is no timetable when it comes to grieving; it is a gradual process, and it cannot be forced. It is better for it to come gradually, and one should not try to ignore the pain or keep it from surfacing because it will only make things worse, and the grief process will take very long.

One will feel sad, frightened, and lonely while grieving. These are normal reactions when it comes to loss. If you cry, it doesn't mean you are weak; it is just a normal response to sadness. If you don't cry, you may also sometimes feel the pain deeply. There is no specific time frame for grieving, and the time frame differs from person to person.

Moving on and Looking to The Future

I learned that moving on means accepting your loss, but that's not the same as forgetting. You can move on with your life and keep the memory of someone or something you lost as an important part of you. In fact, as we move through life, these memories can become more and more integral to defining the people we are.

In some cases, depending on who you are, if you lose a partner, you may want to take another partner, but it would not be a substitute for what you had.

You may throw yourself into working, traveling, getting involved with another person, or focusing on something your loved one was doing.

For me, I focused on all the things that my husband was working on and that we were working on together. I can sincerely say they all provided a temporary easing of my pain because when a project was finished, those feelings of hurt and longing came back all over again.

Another situation related to moving on is a feeling of companionship.

I can honestly say that I had and still have a need for companionship, and I still want it, spiritually and physically.

I want to talk to someone other than God. I want to laugh. I want to meet people, not just any type of people, but those I can feel comfortable with and not have to justify my actions and comments.

The feelings of wanting sexual intercourse and physical comfort do not dwindle away immediately, and that longing to be with my husband made it harder to forget the time we spent together.

Sometimes, I would lie in bed and pretend my husband was lying next to me, and it would feel real. Then came the reality check that I was in bed alone.

For men, I learned from some of my male friends whose spouse or partner passed away that the urge for intimacy did not go away after the death of their loved one. In fact, the thought of being alone made them feel lonely, and it got worse as time went on.

Sometimes, they would settle for a woman because they wanted the physical connection and did not want

to be alone.

Coming to terms with reality

We must come to terms with reality and understand not wanting to be bothered. Death means it is the End, it is finished, and there is no coming back. Obviously, Jesus Christ is an exception. I am talking about the physical death that occurs all around.

We have to remember that with support, patience, and effort, one will survive grief, and in due time the pain will lessen, leaving one with the cherished memories of their loved one, but it does not go away totally.

Death is an uncomfortable subject

I learned that death is an uncomfortable topic. Most people would prefer not to talk about it; it is a subject that is either avoided, ignored, or denied.

However, this topic must be discussed and confronted since nothing can prepare one for the loss of a loved one. It comes with many side effects, including dramatic emotions, anger, denial, bargaining, depression, acceptance, disbelief, confusion, shock, yearning, humiliation, despair, guilt, and not forgetting sadness.

Death disrupts one's life, especially if the person is the head of the household. For me, it did just that. My sons suffered in different ways, and when I look at my granddaughter, as little as she may be, she was also hurting.

Death stings and is sharp and painful. It is known to be a final event, which is an irreversible final moment. Losing one's loved one is extremely painful, and because of lingering pain, it may feel like one may never get over the grief and hurt.

I am aware that the death of a loved one is very difficult, and our reactions are influenced by the circumstances of a death, especially when it is sudden or accidental. One's reactions are also influenced by one's relationship with the person who died.

Death experience

When I was a little girl, I would go to the burial ground in the village where I was born and watch the men lifting large boxes in the air and walking into the burial ground while others were screaming and hollering.

I was not allowed to cross the burial ground bridge but still could watch on, and when all was done, I went home and continued with my normal life.

Later, my older sister Pamela experienced the death of her best friend Rosemary, who committed suicide. I became sad for my sister because she was very sad. That was my closest and first encounter with death, and as time went on, there came the death of my brother. That was when I realized in my heart that death is a part of life, and I tried to compare it to a tree's falling leaves as a cycle.

When I look at a leaf falling from a tree, I see two things: if I look at the area where the tree fell, there is evidence of new life sprouting out, and the leaf still has life in it.

After laying on the ground, the leaf becomes nutrients for the tree or other trees or plants.

Also, we must see and understand that our life is a cycle, and as one dies, many are born.

Grief is personal and individual, and every person experiences its nuances differently. Your personality, support system, natural coping mechanisms, and many other things will determine how a particular loss will affect you. There are no rules, no timetables, and no linear progressions. Some people feel better after a few weeks or months, while it may take years for others. There may be setbacks during recovery; this nonlinear process can't be controlled.

It's critical that you treat yourself with patience and compassion and allow the process to unfold.

Grief indicators: the common signs and symptoms of grief

It is hard to accept death when in shock and disbelief. You may feel numb and question whether the loss really happened - this isn't unusual. Some have noted their initial reluctance even to notify others of a loss in case it turned out to be untrue. This is a normal reaction, as you are still expecting your person to call, write, or show up, even if, intellectually, you have accepted their death.

Profound sadness is a universal experience that can often lead to feelings of aloneness or isolation, and we sometimes believe that no one can understand the depth of our grief, which drives us deeper into sorrow.

You may feel guilt over things you said or did or didn't and thought you should have. In cases of suicide, many people question whether they could have changed the outcome. Yet nothing can stand in the way of death or a final decision made by someone else to die, and over time, we must acknowledge and accept that. Still, it's challenging to do this in the early days or months of grieving.

When it comes to anger, regardless of how someone we loved died, anger often comes into play. You may be angry with the person for not being with you anymore or with caregivers for not doing more. You may blame God or others.

You may not be able to direct your anger against a specific source, but find that daily, small injustices seem much more significant than they might have in the past.

This is normal, and no one should tell you that you must stop or let go of your anger. That will happen eventually as part of your process on your timeline.

In the case of fear, a loss can trigger anxiety on many levels, including fear of your mortality, losing those you love, and facing life without the person who died. It can include fear of the future and the uncertainty you may now feel about your life's plans, knowing that someone close to you has died.

We often think of grief as purely emotional, but it can also manifest physically. Symptoms can include nausea, fatigue, lowered immunity, weight loss or gain, insomnia, aches and pains, and more. Although it can be difficult, it's essential to do what you can to maintain your health during grief.

Triggering grief

Many things can trigger grief, and when this occurs, the raw feeling returns all over again. These can be things as simple as attending a meeting that you and your loved one attended, birthday celebrations, holidays and anniversaries, and getting together, not forgetting going to church and traveling together.

For me, seeing someone wearing the same type of clothing and using the same type of cologne reminds me of my husband, especially the smell of his home food, which he loved to cook.

I also realize that whenever I hear of the death of someone, which seems to be very often, the feeling of pain and loss returns.

Suffering in silence

One can suffer in silence when there is a death, especially when it is a loved one, for this is a situation beyond our control, and we do not want to discuss it or talk about it to anyone.

I began hiding my emotions, not wanting to share my feelings with anyone for fear that they would not understand how I was feeling. Also, primarily because of shock and hurt, I did not want to hear what someone else thought.

I learned that suffering can intensify your negative thoughts, and the less you let others know how you feel, the more likely you are to ruminate and allow your inner critical voice to spin in your head. I also had to refrain from seeing myself as being weak.

Everyone leaves a legacy behind

There were so many things to learn as I worked through my husband's belongings. From all the notes he made to the letter he wrote his granddaughter on her first birthday to all the thoughts he had written down, even to some of the secrets he did not want me to know.

Some spoke of him in various forms, like the remarks he made when in a conversation or the suggestions he made, not forgetting the one-word answers he used to provide.

He was a teacher, a preacher, and a family man who loved his community, especially his daughter and sons, and when his granddaughter came into the world, no one else mattered. To put this bluntly, our son always complained that my husband undermined his authority where his daughter, London, was concerned.

Grandfather and granddaughter slept in the same bed since London was two weeks old.

Best of all, my husband kept us together, and he made sure we prayed. If he has not taught the family anything else, he taught us to pray. This was evidenced by our sons' obedience when we asked them to pray - they both knew how, and even London knew to pray and still does.

Transformation

After all the hurting, crying, aching, longing for my husband, desiring to hear his voice, longing to see him being happy sitting with his family and friends and speaking his home language freely, I don't forget longing for his touch. None of these will ever occur again, regardless of how much I want them to happen.

Since this is not in my hand and, rather, in God's hand, who I believe in, I have come to the point of reality that I have to make a change in my life, and I feel that it must either be drastic or gradual; however, there must be some form of change for me to survive.

First, I made a list of all the things that needed to be done and began to prioritize them. Unfortunately, everything seemed important, and since my husband was the head of the household, what should I do, especially where finances were concerned? I could not just sit and fold my arms; there comes a point when food is needed, bills must be paid, car care must be completed, and many other things that require physical action must be done.

As for the finances, I know I must prepare to make sure that whatever I have will be enough to survive. This is something I think and think about all the time, especially for my other friends whose husbands have passed on when they were the head of the household, and I hope and pray they will be okay and taken care of.

For me, adjusting my life was a key action. I had to force myself out of bed to go to work and pray every day that my production would improve and that I would not forget to ensure my work was correct, which I can say was not easy.

As I gradually adjusted to my new life, I knew I felt pleased, and I had this feeling that people were looking at me with pity and sympathy rather than as friends as they had been. However, it was my turn to live and make changes and decisions, and more questions came to mind.

Distracting myself was something I did to survive so that I would not think about my husband. I would not allow his death to put me in a position where I came to my knees, so I knew I had to be able to cope with this debt, and every time I thought about him, I had to remember that he was gone and I had to survive.

Doing what I love to do became easier with the encouragement of my church, family, friends, sons, the special pastor, his wife who embraced me, a couple of the mothers from the church I attend, aunts, uncles, and my husband's family, who never left my side.

They have called every day since my husband died to make sure I am doing well, and don't forget to inquire about their nephews' behavior. Everyone became special to me and to many people. I was surprised to learn so many people were praying for me, and all knew not to mention my husband's name because they knew how I felt.

Conclusion

I wrote about some of my experiences because I feel that sharing what I went through might allow readers to understand that you are not alone. After all, as human beings, we must come to terms with death and understand that our life is a cycle. There are two things that we cannot escape.

We were born.

We will die, and no one who was born of a woman will escape death.

Death stings. Death introduces us to the unknown. Death separates. Death comes without introduction. It never knocks on the door and says, "I am coming." It messes up our plans, and no man can control death; regardless of how we put it, it is a part of our life.

I am saying this because we must come to terms with the facts and understand that our life is a cycle.

The Bible tells us in Ecclesiastes 3:1- 4 that everything has a season. "There is a time for everything, and a season for every activity under the heavens: a time to be born and a time to die, a time to plant and a time to uproot, a time to kill and a time to heal, a time to tear down and a time to build, a time to weep and a time to laugh..."

References

Holy Bible

C.S. Lewis

The APA Dictionary of Psychology

www.biblestudytools.com/bible-study/topical-studies/
why-is-hope-so-crucial-to-our-faith.html

www.ingramcontent.com/pod-product-compliance
Lightning Source LLC
Chambersburg PA
CBHW051242120626
46547CB00014B/1755